THE HOPE
WE RISK

THE HOPE
WE RISK

David Lasley • Anne J. Hill • Ali Noël
Maseeha Seedat • JJ Brinski • Brooke J. Katz
Miriam Wade • Hannah Carter • Tasha Kazanjian
Paula Finlay • Natalie Noel Truitt • Mariella Taylor
Mary E. Dipple • Beth Stedman • Savannah Jezowski

PRAISE FOR THE HOPE WE RISK

"This is a painfully beautiful collection, balancing the fear of loss with the hope of eternity."

— Nathaniel Luscombe, Author of *Moon Soul*

"Utterly gorgeous, *The Hope We Risk* is a sensitive dive into grief and the temporary price we pay for love. It offers hope and relatability to its readers unlike anything I've ever read before."

— Stephanie Dunham, Author of *Everything is Okay*

"Desperate hope shines through every poem and story, highlighting God's truth amongst raw, human emotion. But we are reminded that this hope is not weak—it is forged through sorrow, allowing it to be fully embraced and celebrated in its purest, unbreakable form. This book is for those who feel alone in their hardships. It is for those who need the Spirit to move. It is for those who need a holy and healing power in a broken world."

— Emily Barnett, author of *Thread of Dreams*

"*The Hope We Risk* is a beautiful gift to any heart that grieves. These poets generously offer their own pain and vulnerability as a reminder that we are not alone, that there is no one-size-fits-all way to suffer, and that hope is always a risk worth taking."

— Rachel Lawrence, Author of *Seashells & Other Souvenirs*

The Hope We Risk

Paperback ISBN: 978-1-956499-20-9

Published by Twenty Hills Publishing

Cover Art by Lindsey Lasley

Interior Formatting by Stephanie Dunham

Edited by David Lasley, Anne J. Hill, and Elaine Wells

Book created by Anne J. Hill, head of Twenty Hills Publishing,

with the help of David Lasley

All citations of the Bible come from:

New International Version. (2011). BibleGateway.com. http://www.biblegateway.com/versions/New-International-Version-NIV-Bible/#booklist

Content Warnings: Grief, child loss, miscarriage, illnesses, death

David Lasley:

To Maggie Lasley and Beverly Friend, both of whom I suspect would have rolled their eyes, said "Dave!" and been generally embarrassed by the extra attention if they were here to read this. I love you, miss you, and will see you soon.

Anne J. Hill:

To my Grandpa, Robert, to my Grandma, Lois, to my Aunt Cheryl, and to my mom, Karla. You ran your races. You left your marks. You changed my life. I love you all. May you celebrate in eternal peace. To my dad, Geoffrey, for being a steadfast husband to your wife and a guide to all your children, even in the midst of your own grief. I love you.

CONTENTS

THE MOMENT OF

FACING SORROW

FAITH THROUGH GRIEF

INTRODUCTION

I still remember the dreaded "phone call" when I was a freshman in college. My grandma had suffered a heart attack, and they weren't sure that she would make it. I remember numbly, hurriedly driving in a snowstorm up I-55 in the hopes that I'd get there in time. Fortunately, she pulled through. Unfortunately, it wasn't the last, nor the most difficult time I'd have to pick up the phone.

The challenge with talking about grief is that it is easy to either act like everything is ok or to become buried in it. I've personally been more prone to the latter, though I've felt the temptation of the former as well. For me, the only solution to this impossible pendulum swing has been allowing my faith in Jesus to inform my honest grief. This has not been easy, but I have seen God's pursuit of me perhaps most vividly in these dark spaces.

This is why I couldn't say "yes" fast enough when Anne pitched the idea of this book to me. Each of us has a story to tell, and my story involves discovering healing and hope even in the midst of the most terrible circumstances. It's not an easy thing to rehearse, and I don't want to diminish how long and difficult of a journey it has been. In fact, writing this almost feels like a contradiction in terms—how could light and goodness be remotely present in the darkest spaces of my story?

But I think this is the risk. To somehow honestly confront the current bitter reality of death while also pursuing the One who wasn't defeated by it. He "has destroyed death and has brought life and immortality to light through the Gospel," (2 Timothy 1:10, NIV). May the words offered in these pages bring you some measure of comfort and encouragement in that journey.

-David Lasley

————

In recent years, I've buried more family than I'd like to think about. I am no stranger to grief. I used to be, but there's no avoiding it now. It's been just over two years since my mom passed away, the most recent departure in my family. Since then, I've had a few friends go through similar trials. I found some of them asking me questions along the lines of, is this thing I'm doing/feeling *normal*? Should I be concerned? When does this get easier? My answer? There is no normal. Of course, there are obvious reactions that fall into "concerning," but these were "normal" concerns, in the sense that there also is no normal. Everyone handles grief differently and in their own timing. And really, the most help I think I've ever been to someone else grieving is to let them know they're not alone in their grief. Sometimes, that looks like sharing my own struggles.

That's my goal with this book. I want people to know they're not alone. While no one can understand your specific journey with grief, there are many out there who *get* how no one else can *get* it.

And best of all? There is someone who completely gets it. Someone who carries the weight of all our grief, not on His shoulders as if it were only someone else's pain, but in His soul.

That's why we can even begin to risk hoping. It would be so much easier not to hope, to curl up and let the world run by (and some days, that's all we can do, and that's okay, too). But the risk is in not staying there indefinitely. To put on your shoes and step outside your door because there is a life to be lived even if grief hits again.

My hope is that you find comfort in this book. I expect there to be tears (trust me, there were many going into this as well), but tears that water growth and healing. God bless you on your journey, friend.

-Anne J. Hill

PRESENCE AND ABSENCE

Contending with the void
left by our loved ones

WHISPER

Anne J. Hill

> Two years have come and gone
> And you're still not here
> A whisper of a memory
> Thundering in my ears

Today

David Lasley

This day, today, is going to be hard
and there will always be more todays
because grief—it's a punch in the gut—
where you don't fully catch your breath again

And my experience has been
that time doesn't really heal all wounds
because the table's empty chair still greets you
whenever you walk into the room

But we are citizens of Heaven
where we are in a waiting game
looking ahead with expectation
for a different kind of "today"

Where the family meal is not a person short
so our dinner conversation carries later
where all we've lost is recovered, and more,
and we all start finally breathing deeper

Mourning What Could Have Been

Brooke J. Katz

I mourn for what could have been
Tears collected, hugs left rejected
Brushed to the side,
Heart broken

I mourn for someone still alive
Yet twisted and drowned in
Amber liquid

I mourn for the person I wanted
I mourn for a life that was
Never meant to be

God uses the pain and hollow guts to
Grow and strengthen
To help the next generation
Not make the same choices
To break family curses

I mourn for a relationship broken
I lay to rest the what ifs,
The expectations, the unforgiveness

And accepting what is,
Mourning what could have been

NEVER THE SAME
MARY E. DIPPLE

They said I couldn't go back.

I didn't believe them, but now...

Now I know what they meant.

Everything is the same as when I left. The same shutters. The same pink roses Mama took so much care to grow. The same white fence.

But it's all wrong.

It's off.

Empty, like looking at a reflection of what once was.

If I close my eyes, I can remember painting the fence with my little brother. I smile as I remember the way he flicked paint in my face and I chased him around the yard, determined to get my revenge. The way Mama laughed when she saw us covered in more paint than the fence.

When I open my eyes, the memory is gone.

The building is still there. The roses, the fence, the old truck that never ran. They're still there.

But it's not the same.

It will never be the same.

I bend down and carefully snip off a rose from the bush near the fence. I'm careful to do it just right—Mama would skin me if she knew I hadn't—and I walk down the gravel road to the old cemetery. The headstone is cold where my fingers brush its smooth surface and I lay Mama's rose across the top.

"Hi, Mama. I'm home."

My Nieces and Nephews Without Their Grandma

Anne J. Hill

obliviously
they skip and dance
with deep set cares
in things that
don't matter
little feet twirling
past a lineage
they've forgotten
or never knew
with smiles
that can only
come from you
a matriarch
holding them up
nourishing
their very bones
even as they spin
through life
unaware of the footprints
you laid before them

The Walls Cry Out Your Name

Anne J. Hill

The walls cry out your name
The floorboards crave your shoes
The cabinets have an identity crisis
The furniture weeps and sags
The plants search for your sun
The appliances wait for your return
The desk throws itself into a frenzy
The phone can't calculate the lack of your touch
When the heart of the home is torn out
The walls shudder and wail,
"Why have you forsaken me?"
Oh, you of little faith
Someday the walls will be rebuilt
Around a heart that never tears
A restoration that sings from the floorboards
And walls that whisper His name

Remembrance

The moments and people
we won't soon forget

BLEEDING HEARTS

Beth Stedman

Once in late summer
we took watermelons
deep into desert canyons
catapulted them against rocks
with the strength of our arms
watched the red flesh bleed
screamed
when they didn't break we
beat them with sledge hammers
shattering green flesh and
black seeds
upon red rocks
already stained with tears
we thought we could harness the flow
of bleeding hearts
we thought we could channel the pain
of an early goodbye
too early
too soon
too late to say
all that beat in our blood
I love you
I miss you
Goodbye

What No One Told Me

Anne J. Hill

No one told me
I would see you in my sleep
I'd sit with you, sipping tea
Drinking in your wisdom as you speak

But in dreamland's haze
Your words are topsy-turvy
A bewildering dance
Of dreamish riddles

But that's okay
Because I hear your voice
And I see your face
Behind my closed eyes

In the morning,
I make plans to visit you
Before remembering
I can only reach you in my sleep

I struggle to doze off
Because your absence fills my thoughts
But I struggle to wake
Because your presence fills my dreams

Half wishing to live
Half wishing to sleep
This is the plague I like to call:
What No One Told Me About Grief

It Hits Me With No Warning

Anne J. Hill

A picture of your face
Your old purse on the hook
A phrase you used to say
The smell of rain
The kids you helped raise
The ones you never will
A reminder of your embrace
Sitting on your front porch
A song you would sing
Your smile on my face
Something you once told me
Galatians 2:20
A movie you liked
Your voice on my phone
Old cards I wrote to you
The chalkboard we never erased
The dreams you invade
Your chain around my neck
Uninvited memories
Being with family
Rooms you existed in
Rooms you never will
Old fights that flash by
Roads we drove down
Your clothes in my laundry
Mother-daughter characters
Recipe cards you wrote
Your kitchen changing
Visiting others in the hospital
A waft of your perfume

Dating without your advice
A dish on my counter
Throwing away the broken nativity
Visiting your house
Talking about you
Things I borrowed but never returned
Publishing books you'll never see
Stressful tax season
Daydreaming without you
Scrolling through texts
Driving past the hospital
Wednesday mornings
October 13th
Life without you

A Prose Poem for Doug
David Lasley

The receiving line was a surprisingly lonely place. The steady stream of quick, comforting hugs and well-intentioned well wishes felt like it was, well, just that. Just like the kindness of dropping off home cooked meals (mostly lasagna) led to a week of carb and lactose induced lethargy, the repetition of that line left me tired rather than easing my pain. But I didn't complain. I knew there were people there who had driven twelve hours to stand in that line. So I smiled and hugged and nodded.

Until Doug slowly shuffled through the line. I barely knew him except that he was a typical north woods Minnesotan. He liked bears and trees and me and my family and he was there for us, opening his home for Christmas the nine months before this funeral so half of us could have some semblance of normalcy while my sister was in treatment halfway around the world.

Doug leaned in for the normal quick, comforting hug and the same well-intended well wishes just like everyone before him. So I leaned in...only to find that I was giving him a bear hug. And that I couldn't let go. Like puzzle pieces fitting together, something snapped into place in my grieving that I couldn't locate before that moment. I remember weeping like a baby in that receiving line for quite a while.

I barely knew this bear-hugging Minnesotan—why in this forest of people was he the tree on which I chose to lean? Maybe it was because he had not only given the well-intentioned well wishes and had leaned in for the quick comforting hug...it was that long before, he had already leaned in closer.

LINES

Anne J. Hill

We stand in lines every day
Peering down at our shoes
Just waiting for their chance to move
A foot tapping. A sigh
Babbles from a babe too young to know
The difference about this line today
Chatter and hugging old friends
Tight smiles and pats on backs
A "How've you been" so casually thrown
And caught with an "I've been better. You?"
Shoelaces untied, bent to tie them back
He loses his spot as people pass by
A walk down memory lane we all must take
There's no avoiding what's at the end of the line
A chuckle in my ear, and I'm back to that time
You sat silently observing
Waiting for the perfect
Moment to drop a
One liner
The room paused
Then roared in laughter
The medicine we never knew we needed
Until it was expired and tossed in the bin
And now, as I follow the line of smiling faces
It's my turn to step into the room

A fog pummels me,
Thick with unnatural air
Flowers grown in a hot house scattered around
A patchwork of wood acting like a bed

A suit keeping you from being exposed
As if you're there to care
A peaceful smile lifted on your face
Fake
Fake
Fake
I want to scream
An impostor has taken your skin
And spun it into this lifeless thing
Stretched out, and contorted to look like
Someone might be home
And as if the shutters were to reveal the windows
There will be light on inside
A joke nestles on your lips
One unsaid in your final breath
And I watch you, waiting for this to be the joke
For you to sit up, grumble a
One liner
That we all almost miss
The closer I look
The more I'm sure
The flowers are
Fake
Fake
Fake
So I peer at my shoes as I move through the line
On my way to someday end up here again
Because it's a memory lane we must all travel
But you cheated death as your one last prank
You looked to the Heavens, and shouted your
One liner
"I'm coming home, at last!"

Peeling Pictures

Mariella Taylor

    Separating echoes once again.
    Pulling apart each picture,
    reattaching tape to my paper hearts.

    I'll create a majestic shrine
    from the peeling
    faces and damaged shots.

    That way I'll always remember,
    the feelings they forgot.

THOSE NIGHTS

Natalie Noel Truitt

At five years old I asked my mom to make you go home.
In my mind you were a nuisance,
An annoying shadow,
Someone who asked too many questions
And wanted to play all of my least favorite games.

At ten years old you became one of my best friends.
We had realized that we were complete opposites
But that it was okay
And that complete opposites could
Still scream to Taylor Swift at the top of their lungs
And keep each other's secrets for twenty years.

At fifteen years old life was hard.
But it was easy to go swimming
And watch *Friends*
And laugh so hard that we were crying.
We had the same favorite songs
And shared so many favorite memories
I believed that we were invincible
But you knew that we were not.

I was with you when you found out
you were going to be a mom.
You were with me on my first day of college.
We watched each other grow up
But only one of us gets to grow old.

At twenty-four years
I'm left with these memories, pictures, and videos
That will never be enough to make up for the gaping hole
That you have left in my life.
I would give anything to have one more of
Those bright summer Nights
With the hope and the laughter.

Because when I look at your picture
You aren't looking back.
But I know that when you were laid to rest
At the river and the flowers are scattered around
That you aren't here, but you are somewhere far away,
Singing praise to Your maker that you found a week
Before you were taken away.

Seemingly infinite years later I look up at the sky,
And the mix of color reminds me of a painting
You would have painted back in my kitchen
At three am while you laughed until you cried.
And I know that you are okay.

HUGS

Hannah Carter

Sometimes I think of everything we used to do
Those long days, loud laughs, the best hugs
If I close my eyes, I can see it all so well
Do you remember it, even from Heaven?

Painting in your bedroom, staining my hands red
We crafted tiny Christmas trees and homemade boughs
When you tried to teach me how to cook
Burnt mac n' cheese and smoke drifted down the hall
(That was the day I learned that plastic was flammable)

I go back to New Year's Eve
Playing video games and watching TV
All the books you gave me to read
I didn't tell you how much your ghost stories scared me
(That was why I nudged you awake that night
Though you told everyone I threw my book at you)

After you died
Someone told me to write you letters
Pretend you'd read them and smile
Maybe it was supposed to make me feel closer to you
Except I think it just made me cry

I know you're here in spirit
Though I wish you were here in skin
Because I can write you a room full of letters
But I really need to hug you again

OUR PLACE

Mariella Taylor

Fresh cement
poured next to mine
on a walkway into Heaven.
Or at least that's what we called it.

Little handprint
stuck next to mine
building a walkway into Heaven.
Or at least that's what it looks like.

Long ago dates
scrawled into gray mud
on a walkway into Heaven.
At least it will help us remember

Grandpa's grave
stuck at the end
of our walkway into Heaven.

He told me he would be fine.

I'M SORRY

Mariella Taylor

"I'm sorry."
I can see the pain, the rejection, the betrayal
still reflected in your granite eyes,
their harshness reflecting the walls you build
and the wedges I so continually drive between us—
unpurposefully so on my part, I swear it.

"I'm sorry. For all the hurt I've caused you."
But you give me no answer,
and once again all I hear is your silent judgment
made clear through the firm set of your lips,
twisted with your everlasting contempt.
So many times I tire,
and ponder submission to your hatred.
What I have done—it is not purposeful, I swear it.

Standing here before you, I know,
this is my last chance to say anything
to say *something* that might crush this wall, fill this divide,
fix this void between the two of us.
Thorny stems pierce through crinkling
wrapping into my palm,
and I look down at my feet,
gripping tight this gift of roses brought.
As I stand at the foot of your grave,
what words may sum up agony?

LEGACY

Anne J. Hill

What a rich legacy you left behind
Cultivated, a loyal gardener
Pillaging weeds and spraying water
From dawn to dusk, busy at work
Hands browned with dirt
Brow wet, and knees tired
A bed of flowers sprouting new life
Rising up to call you blessed
And in your final surveillance of this garden,
You are washed clean with a
"Well done, my child..."

THE MOMENT OF

The time of passing and soon after

The Time Bomb on the Table

Maseeha Seedat

Thursday afternoon they said
You were back from the hospital.
A check up the following day
Then you'd be free to do as you will.

It wasn't until the weekend I called
Home to ask what had been wrong.
"Everything's fine," they reassured.
"This is what happens when he's lived so long."

Sunday night. My phone rang just before the sun set.
I picked it up. Things don't look too good.
Just pray. Don't lose hope. The voice was silent
On the other end and my whole world shook.

"I'm fine," I whispered, setting my phone down.
That's when the time bomb appeared on the table.
Sleek, opaque, my face reflecting off the blank display.
I couldn't see a single wire for me to disable.

There was nothing on the bomb. Just a little button
On each side. A single camera on the back.
I don't know why there would be a camera on a bomb.
I stared, watching, waiting for my heart to crack.

I stared at it, stared until all I could think of
Was the constant ticking. The relentless, gnawing void
Clawing into the pit of my stomach.
Thinking of anything and everything to avoid

The single question in my mind.
What happens when the bomb goes off?
I stared until the stars came out and the world finally slept.
Then it beeped. More like a melody. Soft.

A gentle, tinkling song in the silence.
My whole body trembled as the melody
Filled the room. I didn't know if it was real
Or my head playing with me.

I lifted the bomb to my ear,
Pressed the call button.
"Hello?" I said
Staring at the pixelated surface.
A string of apologies and then,
"He's no longer with us,"
My father said on the other end.

To Let You Go

David Lasley

To be read while listening to "Ain't Too Proud To Beg" by the Temptations

When I left for
the hospital,
I wasn't planning to
listen to the Temptations
on repeat
for 2 hours straight.

But the wet winter snow
thickly blanketed
everything in sight
and so I couldn't let go of
the steering wheel
long enough to
change the CD
for fear of
losing control.

I was hurrying to
see you, albeit slowly
in that snowstorm, because
I was driving in
my small rusty red
pickup truck.

Like lipstick
streaked across
winter's frosty white face,
I mostly slid
across Interstate 55.

I was white-knuckled, worrying:
would you be there when
I arrived?
Or would my worst fears,
like the howling winter wind
that was chasing me along,
come true?

Thankfully that day's
heart attack
wouldn't take your life.
Though not long after,
I'd rush to the hospital
again. But that time
I had to try
somehow to
let you go.

And I've been trying ever since.

But even though my
small, rusty red pickup truck's
been sold and my
Temptations CD has
long since been
stored away
and you've
long since left me to

grace Heaven's gates
where I imagine Motown
gets plenty of play,
I still find that

    I refuse to let you go.

I FORGOT TO GRIEVE

Anne J. Hill

I was sitting at work
On that couch cushion
The one that nobody likes
The tv blaring some show

I worked in a home
Caring for people
Day in and day out
But tonight was different

You were in hospice,
In groups of two
We came to see you
The day before
We prayed over you
And sang songs

You breathed deeply
Silent but maybe still aware

So very still
Like maybe you'd
Already gone
But forgot your body

I was at work
When something
In my chest
Snapped

I looked at my phone
And there was the text
You were gone
Slipped away

I didn't cry
I didn't tell
Anyone at work
I wasn't surprised

I sat there on that bad cushion
The tv blaring some dumb show
And was glad you were in a better place
With no more pain

The last days had been hard
The cancer taking you over
I prayed you would go
To be with Peaceful Grace

I think I did cry, eventually
When it set in
But death had started to become
Normal in our lives of late

And I miss you
I think of you when
I drink coffee from
The mugs you made

Or when I decorate for Christmas
With the ornaments you created
The pictures on my walls you painted
You would have loved my cat

I lived in your home after you passed
It was surreal
And sweet
And brief
Just a body to fill the space
Where yours used to be

It was too quiet, alone
And I guess maybe it had been for you too
Or maybe you got used to the silence
Filled with three cats chasing around

My cousin lives there now
And I forget the home was yours
Until I'm there alone and it falls still

I can almost see you at your desk
Creating beautiful art
Praying with passion
Opening your home
To the lost and forgotten

You were a wonderful aunt
And I've realized
I forgot to grieve
Out shadowed by my mom's slow passing
If I didn't cry before,
I am now

And I'll see you again someday
With my mom, grandma, and grandpa
But for now,
I'll think of you
Every time I drink coffee

Then, Again,

David Lasley

> I saw the
> three missed calls
> and the flurry of
> texts with the
> two frantic words
> repeated across
> my glowing screen:

> "Call me."

> Then, again,
> I relived
> every previous emergency
> sorted neatly in my
> mental Rolodex
> to satisfy my
> persistent
> fear complex.

> Finally
> (years and
> minutes later),
> I held the
> phone to my ear
> while I held my
> anxious breath
> waiting to learn what
> I wish could've
> just been
> hidden from me.

The words
washed over me
like a cold rain
on those
frigid days where
it wasn't quite snowing
and every drop felt
like a personal
assault on joy,

Yet again,
I was mistaken
to think that
my hope was that
You would
hide me far from
tragedies like this.

Then again,
as disappointing as that was,
I was
truly grateful that,
You would
hold me close
then, again,
and forever.

BEAR WITH ME
ANNE J. HILL

You forget things when you're just trying to remember how to breathe again. Like what time to be at work, or how to crawl out of bed, or that you're *not* supposed to tell people the truth. The truth about how she died.

"It was peaceful," they say. It's the story that's tossed around. "We all got to sing to her as she passed away." Which is true. "We all got to be there, tell her goodbye." Also true. "They let us all in her hospital room, even during Covid." Again, true. "She didn't struggle much." Partly true.

But we don't deal in part truths, apparently. We pick the better half, the easier one to swallow and digest and go about life with. That's the one we tell.

I didn't realize this. I thought honesty was called for.

So when they asked what it was like, and she said, "She didn't struggle much," I interrupted with, "Yes, she did. She was struggling to breathe." I would have gone on, but when I got *that* look to shut up, and the hearer's commonplace face twisted into second-hand trauma, I stopped.

It makes sense, I guess. No need for anyone else to endure what we did. Or maybe some of us are better at forgetting certain details than others. Or we try to block them out and pretend it works. But

I can't. I've tried. But then, there she is. Gasping. Cold. I'll spare you, as I've been quietly ordered to do.

But it wasn't peaceful.

Yes, moments were. There is a lot I'm grateful for. It could have been much, much worse. But the blessings of that late night/early morning don't take away the memories I'm supposed to forget. They never will.

They're seared, core memories.

Things a person's body was never meant to endure, lodged into my brain. And most of the time, I've forgotten. Until some nights when I lay down to sleep, and I'm affronted with images that only grow clearer the harder I shut my eyes.

It's not beautiful. This was never meant to happen. Death was never meant to plague us. It was never meant to take her from me. Or to throw the world into unhinged chaos. And yet, here we are. Facing death, an end of the road, one way or another.

I'm not hopeless; please don't get me wrong. Hope and faith are all I have left. But I'm angry. Angry that death thinks it has a place on this Earth still, when I know better. Because she isn't dead. God looked death in the face and bled.

So we can spend an eternity in joy. Real, unadulterated joy. Not plastered smiles, and fake "I'm okays."

But for now, pardon me if I sometimes say too much. If, sometimes, I pretend I'm okay. If I cry at a wall. If I force a smile on Mother's Day. I'm not perfect, and sometimes, I'll forget how to breathe.

Bear with me.

Maggie - A Sonnet

David Lasley

My sister, wife, and I went out that day—
A simple trip for clothes—until we heard
My phone, then our own cries, receiving word
That Maggie died while we were still away.

When looking back, perhaps we should have stayed
Away, our happier memories preserved.
But…"they'd leave her out for us," the Home assured
So she laid still, ling'ring there in wait.

The Funeral Home thought she would calm our woes,
But she had gone to Heaven's sweet release.
We traveled back so fast in faux suspense
As if somehow the weight of grief and sorrows:
Her presence there, so partial, could have eased.
She was still there—and yet—it made no difference.

The Door to the Unknown

Anne J. Hill

I laid in bed, just ten years old
Watching the door to the unknown
Tucked away in the attic
Of Grandma and Grandaddy's house
It used to be a window and now
It's a not-so-secret passage
I dreamed it led to far off lands
Of magic and wonder and delight
Or when the shadows danced,
That it brought horrors from beyond
My imagination running wild
Sleep evaded my little eyes
And down the stairs I'd run
To the safety of their arms

I laid in bed, twenty-something years old
Waiting for the alarm to ring
And summon me to your side
Grandma needed help at midnight
Taking turns, swapping shifts
Watching you slowly fade
I wonder if you dreamed
Of magic and wonder and delight
Or if the fears of slipping away
Made you want to cling on tight
In the end, you opened the door
To a place you'll see His face
In the safety of His arms
Where all fears and sorrows
Are crushed beneath His feet

The Journey

Paula Finlay

Your bags were packed, though rather light,
for the journey you would take

Your heart, just wanting to let go,
so full of grace and strength.

This earthly world you once clung to,
no longer held you here.

Your face, it glowed with realization
of meeting friends so dear.

My sadness contained, I whispered,
"It's okay to leave."

Not fully understanding once you left
how much I'd grieve.

IT'S NO EASY THING

Ali Noël
  content warning: miscarriage

It's no easy thing
when two conflicting emotions
coexist within the soul
When relief and grief spring
from the same well
In one night, I lost my baby
but was spared the grave
and it's always been a tricky thing

The doctor yelled *she's going!*
right before it all went gray
This is so unfair
my last thoughts
as the faces of my soon-to-be-grieving children
and family
ran across my mind

Then a promise made to Joshua
met me in the dark
Whispered into my collapsing soul
Don't be afraid, Ali, don't be discouraged
for the Lord your God is with you
wherever you go

I'll never forget waking up
to realize
It's not my turn to die
Shouts and lights and wires and blood
I'm still here

Grateful, relieved
but the night wasn't over
I'd made it through mercy's door
but grief still waited in the hallway

In the same breath
I grieved my miscarried son and
thanked God for
allowing me to see the sunrise

Truly, He is with me
wherever I go
Even though I still get scared

Truly, He is with me
when discouragement comes

But it's no easy thing

FACING SORROW

Navigating the
difficult journey of grief

Have You Ever

David Lasley

The Day

I wonder—
have you ever had to
watch as someone died?

To lean in
whispering, "I love you"
before you said, "Goodbye"?

To feel death's
heavy emptiness
pressed upon your bones

As you watched
the blinking monitor
and heard its final tones

Have you ever had to
suddenly feel
a little more alone?

—

The Next Day

I wonder
have you ever had to
wake up the next morning?

And try to somehow
stumble through the day
while you're still mourning?

To watch as
people sped on through
their very normal days

And all the while
you felt so numb
your feet got stuck in place

Have you ever had to
watch them moving on
while you're delayed?

—

A Year or So Later

I wonder
have you ever had
to finally face your dread

Of everything
collapsing in
again
upon your head?

To risk a smile
when all the while
those ghosts kept crawling near?

You'd hesitate...
you'd wait for joy
to slowly disappear

Have you ever tried to
hold to hope
a little tighter than your fears?

—

15 Years Later

I wonder
have you ever had
to try to live again?

(Like, *really* live
though of course
it'd never be like it was back then)

To somehow grieve
this loss but see
there's still more here to gain?

And fight to build
more memories
despite the searing pain?

Have you ever had
To choose to love
And live this life again?

—

Someday Soon

I wonder
have you ever had
a longing unexpressed?

To feel these
heavy burdens
on your back get laid to rest?

Where loved ones
in this world are not
just momentary guests

But living
breathing memorials
of the Savior in your chest?

Have you ever
really longed for
the dead to resurrect?

BRAVE

Beth Stedman

Brave is a hospital room
cold floors
sterile bed
thin blankets
the steady drip of an IV's hum
a lulling melody
echoed by the sound of nurses
talking in the hall
laughing as if all is well
while you drink cheap coffee
in the dark
trying to stay awake
to watch
to wait
for the unknown
that may
or may never
come

To the One Who Grieves

Ali Noël

Someday you'll see it again
the stardust outside your window
the fairies by the stream
the magic in the snowfall
Someday

THE THING ABOUT DREAMS

Savannah Jezowski

The thing about dreams,
You see,
Is they begin in the light,
In sweet musings and blissful contemplations.

But they're twisted in the night.
They change,
Mangled, ugly reflections
Of what they were born to be.

The other thing about dreams?
They don't last.
The nightmares fade
And new beauty begins with the dawn.

THE KITCHEN

David Lasley

The smell of
Baking cookies
Drifts out from the kitchen

Rich chocolate chip
Mixed with sugar and butter
Every bite sweeter and softer

It couples with
Inviting sounds of
Joyful laughter

Turns out they scattered
The powdery white flour
Absolutely *everywhere*

And I am covered in the
Aromas and tones
Of unbridled joy and goodness

While I sit out here in
My comfy, beige chair
Adjacent to the kitchen

I confess that I have also
Often kept hope
At a fairly comfortable distance

But the scent and resonance of
A butter-rich dessert and a
Laughter-full room

These irresistibly (un)common graces
Generously beckon me
To head back into the kitchen

BY PRECARIOUS STEP

Ali Noël

I don't like being here
on this rickety bridge of
anguish-frayed rope, loss-weathered planks
never knowing when
sorrow's wind will blow

Despair's jagged chasm waits beneath
and I've crossed enough bridges
to know
those broken pits
aren't where I want to be

Rope-burned hands, wood-cut shins of heartache
are manageable
but another climb out of that suffering abyss
will take more than I've got
to give

Going forward risks a fall, but
I can see no greater loss
than to build my house on Grief's bridge
so step by precarious step
I go

THE HOPE WE RISK

David Lasley

It's leaning in to feel
The pain—to let it heal
And trusting that it will
That is the hope we risk

To know it's not a fake veneer
To let a smile appear
While our eyes still fill with tears
That is the hope we risk

While feelings ebb and fade
It's toiling still to pray
With no words left to say
That is the hope we risk

It's trusting what we know
He aches to come in close
So where else would we go?
He is the hope we risk

ABLAZE
ANNE J. HILL

Grief hits me like a burst of flame. It begins as a spark, a fire yearning to set ablaze. Smoldering, disintegrating into a pile of ash. The smallest encouragement wakes it up, even in the dead of night when I hear whispers of your melody in the stars. It steals all the oxygen from my lungs. I stand on the edge of Heaven and Hell and wonder which one I might fall into. The precipice of blessing and insanity.

I'm not being dramatic. Just grasping for the words to explain that feeling when my chest locks up and breathing evades me. When all I want is to slam my fist on the cobblestone countertop, but I don't like pain, so I won't.

But I could.

I could burn the world with one fist and a few words.

But I won't.

A world so tragic and lost, spinning around in space like it has somewhere to be, but it always returns home.

Like my heart, banging against my chest and smashing into my lungs. Maybe if it tries hard enough, it can break out of this cage of flesh and soar up to the sky where you are.

But it can't.

I close my eyes and imagine a place where everything is right.

Where people mean it when they say they're okay. Where everyone's hearts are on their sleeves, and there are no secrets left unturned. A utopia of sorts—the kind where you're allowed to feel and be unique. Not the kind where everyone falls in line and uniformity is praised.

But we're not perfect.

So bring me back to this Earth. In a time where pain is felt and sometimes hidden. Because this is the smoke-filled reality in which I breathe and where embers glow. There is no other planet for me. No stars that can sing.

But there will be someday...

A CRY

Anne J. Hill

Bravery is for the weak
The ones who cower
In the dark
But hold a candle
And whisper
"Help me"
Despite the shadows

Dear Grief

Ali Noël

> like a wave of the sea
>   take my heart
> slam it against the shore
>   and watch
> as all the glittering pieces
>   spray across the sand
> like shattered bits of shell
>   once used to house life
> how fitting, how sad
>   but, maybe, when the time comes
> I'll dig into the depths
>   and there may be treasure yet
> beneath the seascape
>   of this broken heart of mine

HURRICANES

David Lasley

> What do I do
> when I'm dreaming dreams
> the size of hurricanes
> but all I get are
> drops of rain?
>
> Let it rain.

MOONBEAMS

Savannah Jezowski

I didn't want this,
This valley of shadows,
Of painful things
And fears
And dark, lonely nights.

I didn't know love
Could hold so much pain.
How can something so small,
So fragile,
Bring so much fear?

You fit in my hands,
a tiny thing with feeble cries.
Yet you fill my world,
Drowning out
The call of the ordinary.

But darkness has its beauty:
The glow of moonbeams,
Whisper of twilight winds,
The shadows
A gown of security.

For with each shadow
Also comes a sunbeam.
And every darkness holds
A memory
Of triumph over fear.

THERE ISN'T MUCH TO SAY
ANNE J. HILL

The lady says she's sorry for Landon's loss, and he nods a few times, mumbling his thanks. Then there's an awkward pause that feels drawn out but really must just be a couple of seconds, and the lady adds, "There isn't much to say," with a sad, knowing smile.

Landon nods. "I know." He nods again.

There's a lot of nodding at funerals.

Then she walks away and leaves Landon standing there alone in a crowd of strangers. He knows she must have also loved his sister, just like all the other unfamiliar faces dabbing their eyes and muttering goodbyes.

And he knows she didn't mean it because there *is* a lot to say. Too much to say. Too much to fit into a superficial conversation.

In the auditorium, friends that Landon has never met and distant family he hasn't seen in years gather as the pastor leads them in prayer—a heavenly thanks for her life. Pictures of her time on Earth dance on the wall, and they try to share, to remember, to laugh as she would have. But there's too much to say.

It's Landon's turn to speak, but his legs won't allow him to stand. A heartbeat later, his orphaned niece pokes his arm, and his feet are moving him to the stage.

But he doesn't have much to say. To tell everything he misses, everything he's feeling, everything he's thinking would take too long and hurt too much, and there's a schedule to keep. If he were to go overtime, his sister would ask where she could submit an official complaint ... if she were there.

They all nod as Landon talks because, even though they might not have been around for the stories he's telling, they can still picture her obsessive organizing and unique displays of love, because they apparently knew her, too.

Then it's over. All of it. And they make Landon and his family walk down the aisle to leave—exchanging teary smiles and nodding heads with the seated crowd. Landon reassuringly squeezes his little niece's hand. He's responsible for her now.

And there's too much to say.

A laugh pierces the heavy air as shoes plod through the sludge outside. It's been snowing, so the grass is muddy. Another laugh. They do it because they'll cry otherwise, and they've already done that inside.

The dearly departed's childhood friend says some words over the coffin. It's hovering above a hole, just waiting to become one with the dirt. People nod, and chuckle, and cry.

And there's too much to say, but not enough time.

Soon, too soon, she's asleep in the ground. But a thought strikes Landon's heart—something that went unsaid for most of the day. She's not truly asleep. She'll never need sleep again because that's just her body. Her soul is somewhere else entirely, laughing in controlled bursts and organizing the seasonings in the kitchen, if they have those in Heaven.

As cars drive away, Landon helps his family clean up, focusing on what needs to be done. He can cry again later, but for today, his eyes are tired. So, he acts like they're just tearing down tables from a casual party—the kind his sister would have loved to plan.

And he nods and smiles because someday, he'll have plenty of time to say everything that needs to be said.

I HEAR YOU

Savannah Jezowski
content warning: child illness

As the oxygen hums
I hear you breathe,
Each breath a rattle
Promising long nights,
Long hours in the darkness
A sick accompaniment
To the song of your stridor.
How many nights we will listen
To the sound of your breaths,
These squeaks and snorts
That whisper premonitions
Of dark things,
Of no breaths.
Please, God, anything but that.

I hear you cry,
That breathless keening,
Such a wail,
That screams, "My belly hurts,"
The feeding tube gouging into your stomach,
Too tight, way too tight.
You puke
And puke
And puke
And I wonder if it will ever end.
They said it would be a good thing,
No tube in your nose,
But this tube in the belly...
It's a different kind of hell.

How I long to hold you close,
To my breast,
Caring for you the way a mother should,
The way a mother needs to,
Skin on skin.
But I mustn't do this, they say,
Aspiration and choking,
So it's the hole in your stomach.
At least it's better than no food at all.
Thank God for mixed blessings.

I hear you sleeping.
When did the squeaking stop,
That adorable snuffling
I didn't even know I was missing?
When did you start sleeping through the night,
Quietly, peacefully,
The way a baby should sleep?
When did *I* start sleeping through the night,
No phantom cries, no ghostly echoes,
Only peace and faith
That dawn will come.
It always comes.

WHERE DO YOU PUT THE GRIEF

Beth Stedman

where do you put the grief
of living
when it overflows the cavity of your chest
how do you hold the years
of loving
when they weigh a lifetime
what do you do with the hurt
of the world
when pain surges through your blood
how can we push the darkness
back
into the box our soft hearts opened
where do you put the grief
how do you hold it
here

FAITH THROUGH GRIEF

Hopeful words and honest prayers
in the midst of pain

Kintsugi

Tasha Kazanjian

I can follow the line with my mind
a delicate stroke of black stretching
out from the bullet hole
a single hair snapped from a bowstring
and singing out a thin note of pain.
But the line grows into a ravine
a fever of vertigo when I near the edge
and if I push myself close,
testing my weight against the rim
my thoughts crumble into the empty space
my breath jerks and scrapes like a sour violin
and I don't know what will happen
if I lose my balance.

A hundred cracks lash out
and I learn what bad luck it is to step on them
until my thoughts know how to skip
to bend and curve and twist away
how to angle so the ugly fractures
in the landscape of my mind
never appear in the picture.

But when I look at You, I have to look at them, too
look at the fragile, beautiful thing You created
and hold up the broken pieces
shards that cut into my fingers and leave rusty stains
wherever I try to disappear.

You take each splintered fragment.
Your hands are calloused and soft
hurt and whole
but even when You bring the pieces back together
I can still see the pale threads of the cracks.

Until You trace them over
mercy made of fire-bright resin
a honeyed lacquer sealing away the scars.
The hollow places crossed out in rays of molten light.
You hand my heart back to me
anointed in gold

5:03PM IN GLOOM CITY, MI

JJ Brinski

Fog squats down on my
town like a sumo wrestler
in a smart car. And I sit
tired and weatherworn
inside this bike shop, with
Dylan and The Dead in my
ears. Never really listened
to too much of either.
I drop my 43-year-old
head into my hands and
ask the Father of Fogs
just how—precisely—am I
to "practice resurrection"
in this half-gone Holy Week?
How? When another has died,
young, in-prime, and my
griever is grievously tried,
How? When I can neither feel
nor see your smile through
drowsy clouds, lethargic,
crying all over the pages
of truth.

Resurrect me. Let me practice
while you preach me to life.

Not How I Had Hoped

Anne J. Hill

I prayed for healing
A mending of your body
An extension of your life
So you could stay a little longer

But God took you home

Some prescribed more faith
More prayer, more petition
A simple equation of belief
That always leads to the outcome we seek

But the God I know is not so limited

God's will be done,
I prayed through tears
Because sometimes His plans
Look like taking a daughter home

But I still wish God had left you here

My prayers were answered
Just not how I hoped
But your body is healed
And your soul set free

You've finally reached home

And sometimes I'm jealous
Of your new closeness to God
How you see His face
And He holds yours

An eternity with your Healer

So until I join you at last
I'll remember God's grace
In saving your soul and
Healing your broken body

Greater peace than I can fathom

—*Thank GOD that He isn't bound by the level of my faith. If He was, He'd be following* my *shortsighted plans, and that would fall stupidly short of His vast sovereignty.*

BETTER DAYS

David Lasley

I want to try to see Your dream
of better days that warm and gleam.

A rising sun o'er calming seas,
pelagic colors, a gentle breeze.

But all I see's the pounding rain;
this dark and wild hurricane.

It bows me low. I grit my teeth
to fight from being pulled beneath.

But my despair's an anchor weight.
My grief would say "accept this fate."

Perhaps if you would buoy me
Then maybe I could sail this sea

And navigate these perils through
And dare to hope your dream is true.

OH SOUL OF MINE

David Lasley

Everything's uprooting here,
the ground beneath me heaves.

My chest is slowly tightening now,
my heart more quickly beats.

Oh soul of mine, so grieved and weary,
be quiet now and rest.

Be like a sleeping child, leaning
on their mother's breast.

Oh soul of mine, so grieved and weary,
let God give you His rest.

Phenomenal Cosmic Power, In an Itty-Bitty Living Space

JJ Brinski

You are deep and wide,
deep and wide, phenomenal
in stride and sized not by the
measurements of men.
But that's not the God I need
right now, as captivating as you can be.
No, I need you, breath-brushingly close,
hushed, with comforts of radiant body
heat in embrace. I need your tears
to intermingle with those on my face,
rivulets rushing with hot emotion, salty,
lapping up to my shivering skin's sweat.
I need the wrapping up of one who
burst through grave clothes, un-mummified
and new. Right now I need you small,
and relentlessly incarnate. Oh King of the
Comet-strewn Cosmos, I need you to be
melancholic in majesty,
diminished in stature,
and holdable in holiness.

When I Write

David Lasley

When I write,
I take too long,
I wrestle hard
with what to say
to lay my faith
beside my grief,
but words are slow
to come this way.

I'll quickly write
a dismal lament
a stifling spiral
of despair.
The choice to take
a breath of hope
is a battle, but
I need that air.

SCREAMING

Anne J. Hill

I cry in the car
Windows up
Grief locked in
While driving
(Not advised)
But it just
Happens

I scream in the car
Smack my palm
On the wheel
Like a two-year-old
Who lost a toy
But I've lost
So much
More

I swear in the car
Where no one
Can hear my soul
But my God
Who isn't offended
By a little word
And sees the pain
Beneath

I pray in the car
Eyes wide and
Raging, mumbling words
In spuming, sporadic fits
How could You?
But also
You have the right
But My God
Help me

I sing in the car
Tears stain my lips
My guts spilled out
In the lyrics
Pumping into my veins
Flesh torn open
For no one to see
But me and my
God

A VILLANELLE FOR AMOS

Ali Noël
content warning: dealing with loss of a child

I stand alone before the night
As darkness settles, but I'm not afraid
Beneath the velvety glow of the starlight

The violet expanse, glorious sight
I feel the weight of Love, bigger than myself
Calling me forward, to stand upright

I gaze up at celestial height
Wonder and weariness turn within
Though we're called apart, we'll reunite

The enormity of the heavens, ethereal light
Making my life feel small
The majesty of Your hand, my heart contrite

Basking in the gleam, my chest pulled tight
I hold to the promises of old
That the stars, by name, You alone recite

By faith, with hope, my soul takes flight
Pressing into truth unshaken, hope divine
Your plans for me, peace invites
As my baby lives beyond the starlight

A Prayer, Lament, and Reflection on Psalm 22 in Iambic Pentameter

David Lasley

> *My God, my God, why have you forsaken me?*
> *Why are you so far from saving me,*
> *so far from my cries of anguish?*
> *My God, I cry out by day, but you do not answer,*
> *by night, but I find no rest.*
> *Yet you are enthroned as the Holy One;*
> *you are the one Israel praises.*
> *Ps 22:1-3*

I think that joyful praise in crushing loss
Sounds like a song that's sung out of its key.
I try, but find it hard to hear the sound
Of words that hold such incongruity.

Does faith make light of all my pain and tears,
Enforcing happy tunes on elegies?
No—You were weeping more than me while You
Composed Your resurrection melodies

And it has taken longer than I thought
It would to grow that sort of firm belief,
Accepting when I see You give to death
A permit when you could restrain its grief

And trusting You could lead me into hope
Whether in three months or years or days
Of resurrection power breaking through
When lost ones live and tombstones roll away.

For You are not a stranger to my plight.
In fact, You suffered till Your life was spent.
Still somehow on Your cross You managed praise
To God that harmonized with Your lament.

You who fear the Lord, praise him!
All you descendants of Jacob, honor him!
Revere him, all you descendants of Israel!

For he has not despised or scorned
the suffering of the afflicted one;
he has not hidden his face from him
but has listened to his cry for help.
Ps 22:23-24 (NIV)

AND THIS IS WHY I LOVE HIM

Ali Noël

> *"A bruised reed He will not break and a*
> *smoldering wick He will not snuff out.*
> *In faithfulness He will bring forth justice."*
> *Isaiah 42:3*

When mourning's fists pummel my soul
the One who sees me blackened and bruised
will not break me
the One who sees me desperately hanging on
will not snuff me out

In faithfulness He will bring forth
a generous uplifting out
of what bruised my heart
of what wore me to the wick

And this is why I love Him

Recently, *(a villanelle)*

David Lasley

> I saw his face was worn and tired from the strain
> as an old friend said his sister died in the last few years.
> I shook his hand
> and felt the weight of this broken world again.
>
> I was in a church where a woman explained
> the way her husband was aging beyond his years.
> Her face was worn and tired from the strain.
>
> I went to see Papa at the hospital but I had to remain
> in the car and FaceTime instead (COVID fears).
> Phone in hand,
> I held the weight of this broken world again.
>
> I checked in with my wife about her level of pain.
> She'd had a bad episode but she fought to appear
> as if all she'd faced hadn't worn her down from the strain.
>
> I looked in the mirror to find the weary lines I've obtained
> on my face. I traced those paths for now-faded tears
> with my hands
> and touched the weight of this broken world again.
>
> I prayed alone and sang all my hopeful refrains.
> And as I waited for Hope's face to finally appear,
> I noticed He too was once worn and tired from the strain.
> So I held His hand,
> and He carried the weight of this broken world again.

LINGERS

Miriam Wade

Amidst the light of day and dark of night,
There lies a pain that never seems to cease,
A grief that lingers in the heart's respite,
Which brings a sense of sorrow and unease.

It creeps up unexpected and swift,
And fills the soul with anguish and despair,
A weight that seems impossible to lift,
A burden that we struggle hard to bear.

In every moment, now there seems to be,
Upon our every thought, a shadow cast,
A reminder of the loss that we must see,
A void that we cannot fill or travel past.

But though it may seem endless in its reign,
Time shall heal, and joy shall come again.

THIS DETERMINED, PLUCKY THING

Ali Noël

O, death! Where is your sting?
I'm here to tell you
there's not a place within the soul
death's sting does not reach

I used to think grief,
that snaggle-toothed monster,
would drag me down
beyond Hope's grasp

But here is what I've learned
about Hope
this determined
plucky thing

Loss will beat you to a pulp
heart bloodied, spirit bruised
And just when you think
the monster has had its way

Hope smiles through your broken teeth
Shouting at the beast
O, death! I feel your sting
But I will not let you win

My Darkest Hour

Savannah Jezowski

I am going to drown.
Can anyone hear me?
Why am I left alone,
Adrift in this dark sea?

The boat is going down
so deep into the cold.
My soul is giving up,
Harassed by fears untold.

But then I hear a voice,
Just whispering, "Be still."
The screaming wind dies down,
Bows quickly to His will.

Like a smooth pane of glass,
The water stretches out.
And I'm still in the water—
Is this what faith's about?

Is this what storms are for
So I can hear the voice
Of Jesus calling out
Above the angry noise?

So I can feel His grace
And understand His power
When I am losing faith
While in my darkest hour?

Thrown Stones, a New Alter

JJ Brinski

Stake claim, dear Lord
to this family, to these hearts.
I plant a thinned and threadbare
flag, ragged and whipping in the
stiff wind. To mark. To call down.
To make whatever stand can
still be made.
I am travel-stained and roadworn.
I've done far more weeping
than laughing, more mourning than
dancing. I'm not so sure my feet
remember the steps. The tambourines
are tarnished too, the drumskins dried,
strings have gone rusty, and my
voice remembers not the jubilant
songs of days gone by. On the Maples
there, I hung up my lyre...under the
pines I have wept and wept.
But there must be an end.
I have thrown more stones than
I care to admit, Father. Help
me now gather them up
and build you a new altar.

Though sorrow may last through a decade's
worth of nights, there is joy, and
there are mornings.

DEATH AND ALL OF HIS DREAMS

David Lasley

I'm waiting for the day
When Death and
All of his dreams
Finally die

When the well-worn lines
Etched across
My furrowed face
That show not only my age
But also my worry and rage
At all of his lies

Finally get replaced
And life proceeds
Without one more
Fading hope like
An inevitable evening sky

I'm waiting for the day
When the sun will rise
And he can't keep
My loved ones asleep
For one more night

When God says

ENOUGH

And they wake up
From their starless dreams
While Death and all of his
Finally die

And my grief—
Darkened nightmare's over
And we all
Can finally
Come back to life

ACKNOWLEDGMENTS

First off, thanks to Anne J. Hill for the chance to tackle a topic so close to my heart. I'd been praying and thinking about something in this vein for my poetry and was excited to find she was as well. We discovered that our stories bore striking similarities which only further affirmed my belief that this was a great next step creatively. I routinely felt empowered and challenged as a writer in the best possible ways working with her on this. *Anyone* who has worked with her I'm confident would agree that she has a knack for creating spaces for writers where fun, kindness, humility, and tenacity are the norm.

Speaking of writers, I'm so thankful for the way each of them in this collection shared not only creatively, but also honestly about their wrestlings with grief and hope. I found myself hesitant in the editing process because of this, knowing the vulnerable place they'd put themselves in by letting others into their stories. Thank you! Of course, I was not the only one editing—many thanks to all our editors, beta readers, and everyone at Twenty Hills Publishing. A special thanks to Professor Eric Stachera for encouraging and challenging me in my craft. Thanks to my wife, Lindsey, who generously, patiently reads basically all my poetry and makes it so much better. To Ethan, Samuel, and Cora for cheering for me, inspiring me and praying with me about this project. Finally, thanks to the Giver of Hope, who has shown Himself time and again to be worth the risk.

-David Lasley

———

This book was a tough one to write and edit because of the subject matter. And I am so thankful to all the poets and authors who poured their hearts out despite the vulnerability. It is no easy task to splay your soul to the world. And thank you to the editors who took the time to help mold this book into what it is now—specifically Elaine Wells (who we like to call our Poetry Queen here at Twenty Hills Publishing.) Shout out to the beta readers who pitched in as well! Audra, Theo, and the poets who looked over each other's pieces with praise and feedback.

Thank you to David Lasley for jumping in all the way and helping put together this book. I knew I wanted to do a book like this, but poetry is something I'm still learning to love. So I knew I needed someone more well-versed in the medium on my team. After reading a brief poem on his Instagram dealing with grief that hit me hard, I knew I had to ask him. We'd already worked together in the past and I got to meet him and his family in person a while back. (His wife, Lindsey, made this beautiful cover. Thank you for that, too!) I couldn't have done this book half as well without David's help, so thank you!

-Anne J. Hill

About the Poets and Authors

David Lasley resides in Illinois with his wife and kids. He writes to process through everyday experiences of life and faith. He enjoys reading, watching sports, eating tacos and floating muddy Illinois creeks in his kayak. His poetry can currently be found in several anthologies, including Twenty Hills' *Fools Honor* and on Instagram at @dlasleyramblings.

Anne J. Hill is an author who enjoys writing fantasy for all ages. Her love of words has led to her career as an editor and content writer. She runs Twenty Hills Publishing with the help of her circus performing best friend, Lara E. Madden. She spends her days dreaming up fantastical realms, researching ways to get away with murder...for her books, arguing over commas at the kitchen table, talking out loud to the characters in her head, promising her housemate that she isn't, in fact, crazy, and rearranging her personal library—affectionately dubbed the "Book Dungeon."

Instagram @anne.j.hill.editing
Twitter @AnneJHillAuthor
www.annejhill.com

Ali Noël lives in the greater Seattle area with her three young kids and rambunctious bulldog. If she's not writing or having a dance party, you can find her reading, baking or watching any take on a Jane Austen novel. Her work has been featured in *Z Publishing House*, *SobreMesa Zine* and *Wow! Women on Fiction*. You can find Ali and her poetry on Instagram @the.authoress.life

Born and raised in South Africa, Maseeha Seedat takes inspiration for her stories from the most memorable moments of her life. She's a full-time student and a part-time writer, with her first novel, *The Littlest Voices*, published a year after her publishing debut with Twenty Hills. Her writing ranges from the fun and whimsical to the dark and serious, most of the time settling somewhere in the middle. When she's not writing, Maseeha can be found surrounded by her family and friends, or clawing her way toward a degree in physiotherapy.

JJ Brinski is a poet and flash-fictioner living in Marquette, Michigan in the wildly gorgeous Upper Peninsula on Lake Superior. He does life with his talented wife Grace and four growing daughters and writes in community with the Rabbit Room and Flash Fiction Magic. Having many passions, JJ spends most of his time loving space, theology, collecting typewriters, riding his bike ridiculous distances, making up words, and playfully arguing Star Wars. His lucky numbers are 4, 8, 15, 16, 23, & 42.

Brooke J. Katz is a stay at home/homeschooling mom by day and author/poet by night. Jesus and Lyons tea fuel her. Writing and painting have been a way for her to step into another world and for her work to be an outlet for someone else to find encouragement, or just some time to themselves being lost in a story. She is known to always have a book on her and dropping what she's doing to pray. You can find her on IG/Goodreads @Brookejkatz or her website https://brookejkatz.wixsite.com/brookejkatz

Miriam Wade is a Minnesota local who writes young adult fantasy, adventure, and urban fantasy driven by resilient young women, filled with twisty plots, and garnished with a hint of romance. She loves coffee, playing video games, and riding her bicycle. When she is not writing, she enjoys spending time with her husband, their two young daughters, and their cat. Wade is the author of the award-winning steampunk Arthurian inspired series, *One Sword Saga*, and the forthcoming paranormal urban fantasy, *The Woman of Blythe Manor*, as well as a poet in several anthologies.

Hannah Carter is just a girl who wakes up every day hoping to figure out she's secretly a mermaid. She is the author of *The Atlantis Trilogy*, which includes *The Depths of Atlantis* and *A Twist of Tides*. Hannah's short stories and award-winning flash fiction pieces have been published in various anthologies, and in 2022, she won a Realm Award. In addition to fiction, she also has had over a dozen devotions published. In her spare time, she's either cuddling her cats, reading with a cup of tea, or listening to an absurd amount of Taylor Swift. Connect with her on Instagram at @mermaidhannahwrites.

A lover of old books, history, and theology, Tasha writes fantasy inspired by very real places and times. She can't resist adding a bit of magic to her worlds, but her stories primarily focus on how characters interact with those worlds, wrestling with ordinary human conflicts and emotions. Her short fiction appears in several Twenty Hills anthologies.

Paula has enjoyed writing since she was in 4th grade ... a long, long time ago. Years later, after a near death experience, she and her sister (a talented illustrator) collaborated on a book, *The Bears and the Baby*, and published it in 2012. Since then, Paula has been writing for her personal enjoyment and though poetry is her passion, she has another children's book in the works with her sister. When Paula isn't off in her quiet world of poetry, you can find her hanging out with her hubby and fur babies as well as spending time with her adult children and her sweet grandson.

Natalie Noel Truitt is an aspiring Christian author who spends her days working at the library and adding more books to her to-be-read list. She is often on her front porch drinking coffee, reading a good book, and hanging out with her cat.

Mariella Taylor was raised on fairy lit paths somewhere between the backstreet alleys of Jackson, Mississippi and the jazz infested avenues of New Orleans. She spends her days juggling armfuls of books while trying to reach the top shelves in all the local libraries and spends her nights grumbling at her uncooperative characters. Her writing can be found in *Twisted Grimms: Fairy Tales Retold*, *Whispers From Before: Tales of Myth and Legend*, *Aphotic Love*, *Fool's Honor*, and other collections.

A lover of all things magical, Mary E. Dipple uses her talent of spinning stories to shine a light into the darkness that so easily entangles our lives. She is currently writing her epic-fantasy series, *The Lotus Chronicle*s, publication date to be determined. When Mary isn't slaying the darkness with story, she enjoys spending her days tending her ever growing rose garden, playing with her lovable furry assistants, and writing flash fiction. You can find out more about Mary and her stories by visiting her Instagram @mary.e.dipple_author or website at www.marydipple.com

Beth Stedman lives in Phoenix, AZ, with her husband and two kids. She is the co-host of Fable and The Verbivore, a podcast for writers who read and readers who write. When she isn't writing she's helping other people write, obsessively reading speculative fiction and romance novels, and eating way more chocolate than is healthy for one person to consume.

Savannah Jezowski writes swoony-sweet romantic fantasy under a pen name, with a focus on strong leading ladies and brooding but huggable heroes. An advocate for her Goblin Princess with Down Syndrome, she also features characters with disabilities. When she isn't tangled up in magical curses or drinking pumpkin spice coffee, she can be found weeding her garden, homeschooling her Fairy Princess, and reading books by authors like Maggie Stiefvater, Elise Kova, and Sylvia Mercedes. Sign up for her newsletter today to receive a free book!